Within

Anushree Joshi-Mehendale

BookLeaf
Publishing

Presentation by *BookLeaf Publishing*

Web: www.bookleafpub.com

E-mail: info@bookleafpub.com

ISBN: 978-93-95890-44-1

First edition 2022

DEDICATION

To my younger self (and those who might be lost like her): everything you need is already within you.

ACKNOWLEDGEMENT

I would like to thank my mother for encouraging me to work towards my strengths (and identifying writing as one); my father for encouraging me to dream bigger and work harder; my brother for encouraging me to try new things; and my husband for always encouraging me to steadfastly follow my dreams.

PREFACE

Dear reader:

I'd like to acknowledge that I don't think of myself as a poet, rather just as an observer of life. I started writing my blog 'Unsorted Thoughts' as a way to clear my mind and better understand my life. As time went on, it became more about documenting my own journey through life, and reflecting regularly on my relationships, spirituality, business, and self. As a writer, I found that putting my thoughts to paper allowed me to sort through them, and over time, has led me to discover who I am. I hope 'Within' will inspire you to do the same.

- A

Material Games

In a world where consumerism rules our society,
most want material things so they can flaunt it.
But can we ever look inward, and say to
ourselves,
'If it's not for me, I don't want it.'

This rat race is perpetuated
by forces beyond our control,
like companies churning profits
selling products to make our lives whole.

We're being sold what we don't need
every time we wake up.
My self worth is derived from
more than fancy makeup.

I am a person with values
and a true heart.
The material games never end;
I should've never let it start.

Like This, Not That

Small waist, nice nails, long hair, and more
are expectations put forth by the media and such.
They're unreasonable at times, and often unkind;
all this is really too much.

Be thin, not fat.
Like this, not that.
Cover yourself up,
maybe a scarf or a hat.

You'll either be too large, or
not have enough meat on your bones.
People in glass houses
almost always throw stones.

Words are Energy

Words are energy;
they can create a spell.
Whether they're positive or negative…
your brain can't tell.
Speak words of beauty,
and kindness and grace.
Your mind will believe it,
and eventually you can trace
that every negative thought
which you brought into existence
could've been shot down and cleared
in that very same instance.
Our words give us life;
they are our power.
They can document hatred and strife,
or the beauty of a flower.
Words are energy;
they can create a spell.
Life can be fruitful,
if you use them well.

Clinging to Pain

Sometimes
I feel like I cling to pain,
because it is real,
and because what I went through to 'earn' that pain,
the experience,
was, in one way or another,
transformative.
It's a part of who I am,
of who I've become, after the fact,
and I feel that if I let go of the pain,
I'll let go of the growth and of the change in me too.
I don't want to lose the change,
because whatever happens
happens for a reason.
Cliche,
I know. But it's true, too.
Even if I am in pain over something, I am still OK.
No matter what, I know,
I'm going to be OK.
I've survived 100%
of my bad days in the past,
and I'm sure I'll survive

all but one in the future.
Let's do this my way.

Bad Box

We group all our bad thoughts together, and put them in a box. The little box we have in our head, that we think is separate from everything else… really is at the centre of it all.

A bad box.

That's why when we wake up in the middle of the night from a bad dream, our mind automatically fills first with all the worrisome things.

It's all because of our bad box.

The box of nightmares,
The box of fears,
The box of unreasonable expectations,
The box of your tears.

Blessed Right

You have the blessed right
to curate your own life.
To say what you feel,
and be the 'you' that you like.

Magic, Nonetheless

Our home is our
co-working space.

I sit across the room from you,
sharing the space
but not infringing on each other's.

You are rehearsing. It is
soft, tranquil.
The raga you're singing is enchanting.
Bhimpalasi, I think.
It takes my mind away, to
another place.

I am furiously typing on my keyboard,
focused on my train of thought,
with the occasional sigh, or
aimless glance around the room, until my eyes
are back on the words I'm trying to string
together.

Our eyes travel an independently aimless path,
but once or twice, more if we're lucky,
we catch a glimpse of each other
along the way.

Somewhere in this melodious and harmonious
production,
with your voice scaling beautiful notes,
and my words taking form into something
greater,
we are making magic.
Unrelated to one another's,
but magic,
nonetheless.

We create here,
we practice art here,
and we make memories here.

Our home is our
co-working space.

The Shine

I shine when worn
on the fingers of women who adore me.
They call me their best friend.
They say I'm
priceless
because I make them look beautiful,
but little do they know
that I
am not the source of the shine;
for true beauty
lies within.

To Wallow

No one can be positive
one hundred percent of the time.
Sometimes you're allowed
to be sad.
There is a certain comfort
in wallowing.
To cling to your pain and discomfort,
if only for just a second.
To acknowledge your feelings.
To take in a deep breath and let out a sigh,
or tear.
Even the brightest rays of sunshine
fall dull sometimes.
You're allowed a moment or two
to not be optimistic.
You're allowed
to wallow.

Twenty-seven

Family is the most important thing; cherish your time with them.

Friends who've become like family are the most precious friendships; protect those at all costs.

Hustle culture can be toxic. If you're tired, take a break. You can't pour from an empty cup.

If you can't afford to buy it twice, don't buy it (except real estate; it's okay if you can only afford that once over).

Invest your money. Take control of your finances. Abundance flows to those who are ready for it, so be ready for it.

Your self worth is not derived from money or your career; you, as a person, are unimaginably valuable regardless of how much income you have.

Life is short. Make it count.

Twenty-eight

Go with your gut. It is never wrong.

Inspired action is the key to your dream life. If you feel driven to do something, do it immediately.

Dreaming is free. Dream bigger. There is nothing you cannot do, unless you think/believe you can't.

The power of positive thinking is lost on no one. It is not easy nor possible to be positive 100% of the time. But if you can follow almost every negative/invasive thought with a conscious positive one, it will change your thinking over time.

Slow progress is still progress.

Do not spend your time, effort, and emotion where it is not valued. There are people in this world that would do anything to have you in their life. Those are your people.

Young people are confused and often don't know what they want to do with their life. I didn't. Take 80% of your time early on to figure out who you are (not what you want to do). The other 20% will fall into place faster and with ease.

Work isn't everything. At work, no matter how great you are – you are replaceable. To your loved ones, you are not.

Life is short, make it count.

Unbound

You are not bound
by any thread
or any person
to be someone you are not
at any given time.

You are not bound
to stay who you were
when it no longer feels like 'you'
to you.

You are not bound
to any person,
living or dead,
whom you have outgrown.

You are not bound,
by blood or by relation,
by union or by obligation,
to anyone that you don't want to be with.

You are not bound
to suffer, or
to experience pain, or
to have hardships, or

or to live a life less than you deserve.

You are not bound
to be anyone or anything
you do not want to be.

Perfectionism

Perfectionism
is an excuse;
we say we're chasing it;
when really
we're just running away from our insecurities.

Perfectionism
is a curse;
it gives you the illusion that 'perfect' is possible,
when it is not possible,
nor worth it.

Perfectionism
is a fairytale we tell ourselves,
when we are too scared to accept our truth.

Perfectionism
is the enemy of progress;
it is what will slow you down,
and burn you out
every single time.

The Best Version of You

More often than not, it is our fear that holds us
back,
not our actual limitations, or things that we lack.

Fear of failure is as detrimental as fear of
success,
and trust me, my dear, that both of these exist.

Even after we make a gutsy move,
we question ourselves into oblivion.
Did I make the right call, or do the right thing?
What was the point of this rebellion?

The point, my dear, is to test your limits,
and to be the best version of you.
For if you are not you and I am not me,
the world will miss out on us two.

Win at Being Happy

Learning to find
happiness
in everyday things
means
that there is an abundance of it
in your life on a daily basis.

If you assign happiness
only to a small number of infrequent events in
your life,
that may or may not even happen,
then you'll always be waiting and waiting and
waiting
for external factors
to make you happy.

Consider a perspective shift.

Find happiness in your everyday life
so you can be happy
more often.
Make the mundane
beautiful,
and all the small parts of your day
amazing.

It’s a numbers game,
they say.
So win
at being happy.

Imposter Syndrome

Just when you think you've got it in you
to write something,
to join a gym,
to reach out to someone,
to get up and dance…
this little voice in your head will say,
'You're not good enough;
are you sure you want to do that?'

The voice will tell you,
'You'll never be good enough,
so why even try?'

The voice will pull you back
and snicker,
'You don't deserve any of this,
you're not worth it.'

To that voice I say,
'Sit down.
You are not me.'

Within

Stillness is a concept
not attractive - many will find,
but to crave that sensibility
through space and time
means you're unaffected by the happenings
of the outside and the beyond,
and you're focused, instead
on you; you have found
a sense of peace
that surpasses just ignorance
and enters in the realm of
calmness and collectedness.
So close your eyes,
and take a deep breath in,
because the strength you're seeking
can be found within.

Glorious

There is something immensely liberating
about having a philosophy worth celebrating,
that allows you to make mistakes and start anew
even when you think nothing in this life is for
you.

We all have negative thoughts, I know
but you can wash them away, and blow
them into the wind like seeds in summer
and instead turn your mind to something funner
like a coffee when you're at your absolute
lowest,
or maybe shop for that new polka dot dress…
perhaps you go for a walk through the forest
while the path is wet and the raindrops are fresh.

It can be tangible or intangible,
it's the feeling we're trying to get,
whether it comes from things you hold or do,
as long as you know not to forget
that you are a being of this earth,
and there is much more for you here.
There is room in this life
for everything you hold dear.

So rid yourself of your woes
and your negative trains of thought,
for this life is going to be g l o r i o u s,
whether you know it or not.

www.ingramcontent.com/pod-product-compliance
Lightning Source LLC
Chambersburg PA
CBHW051755130826
49812CB00033B/1168
9789395890441